DK SUPER History

TRAIL OF TEARS

Learn about the tragic forced migration of five Indigenous nations in the 1830s, a journey marked by great hardship, sorrow, and loss

PRODUCED FOR DK BY
Editorial Just Content Limited
Design Studio Noel

Author Lisa Bolt Simmons

Senior Editor Ankita Awasthi Tröger
Editor Hattie Hansford
Senior Art Editor Gilda Pacitti
Graphic Story Illustrator Matt Garbutt
Managing Editor Carine Tracanelli
Managing Art Editor Sarah Corcoran
Pre-Production Coordinator Shanker Prasad
Pre-Production Designer Jaypal Chauhan
Production Controller Rebecca Parton
Publisher Sarah Forbes
Managing Director, Learning Hilary Fine

First American Edition, 2026
Published in the United States by DK Publishing,
a division of Penguin Random House LLC
1745 Broadway, 20th Floor, New York, NY 10019

26 27 28 29 30 10 9 8 7 6 5 4 3 2 1
001–350120–Apr/2026

Published in Great Britain by Dorling Kindersley Limited

HC ISBN: 979-8-2171-2576-0
PB ISBN: 979-8-2171-2575-3

Printed and bound in China

www.dk.com

This book was made with Forest Stewardship Council™ certified paper – one small step in DK's commitment to a sustainable future.
Learn more at www.dk.com/uk/information/sustainability

Contents

Words in **bold** are explained in the glossary on page 44.

History in Perspective

The Trail of Tears is the name given to the forced relocation of five **Indigenous** communities from their **ancestral** lands in the southeastern United States. They were moved to territories west of the Mississippi River between 1830 and 1850. This devastating period affected approximately 60,000 people from the Cherokee, Muscogee (Creek), Seminole, Chickasaw, and Choctaw communities. Learning what happened helps in understanding what injustices took place and how **prejudices** shaped US society.

Many white settlers believed that southeastern Indigenous people were **civilized**. They had adapted to some aspects of European culture, such as style of clothes, farming methods, and approaches to trading. But many settlers still viewed Indigenous people as **inferior** to them.

When the US was a new country, after gaining independence from Great Britain, many white settlers thought they could take land for themselves. In 1803, the US bought a huge area in a deal called the Louisiana Purchase. It made the country twice as big. This land was home to many Indigenous groups with their own ways of running their communities. The US government supported settlers who wanted to take over the land, rather than helping the Indigenous communities.

The forced removal of Indigenous people from their homelands was an **atrocity** that affected them culturally and **psychologically**.

The End of the Trail is a statue by the American artist James Earle Fraser that was made in 1834. The sculpture shows an exhausted Indigenous man on a tired horse. It symbolizes the suffering of the people affected by the Trail of Tears.

Where and when?

The Trail of Tears affected Indigenous people who lived in the southeastern US. They lived in what is now Florida, Mississippi, Alabama, Georgia, and Tennessee. The Trail of Tears was made up of several land routes and one water route across parts of nine states. It totaled more than 5,000 miles (8,000 km). The forced relocation happened in the 1830s.

Who was involved?

The US government was involved in the signing of several treaties and **legislation**. Five Indigenous communities were forced to move: the Choctaw, Seminole, Chickasaw, Muscogee (Creek), and Cherokee. **Militias** and the US Army enforced the relocations. Shockingly, they were often beaten, and some were forced to walk in chains. It is estimated that between 4,000 and 6,000 Indigenous people died as a result of the Trail of Tears.

Think about it

We can learn about the Trail of Tears from **sources** such as military, Indigenous, and government records. Military and government records were written by white men. Why might these give us a limited picture of what happened?

Different perspectives

Different groups in society may have deeply contrasting experiences of events. Official records of the past often only present one side of the story. This means that they can't reflect the experiences of everyone affected. To understand what happened, it is important that we look at events from more than one point of view.

Key Events

WHAT HAPPENED WHEN

The forced relocation of Indigenous peoples faced widespread criticism. However, this did not stop President Andrew Jackson and his government from pressuring Indigenous leaders into signing **treaties** and giving up their land and rights.

1816

MARCH 22

George Graham signs a treaty on behalf of the US with Cherokee chiefs. This treaty changes the boundaries of Cherokee land. It also gives the US the right to open and use roads, rivers, and waterways through Cherokee land.

1825

FEBRUARY 12

William McIntosh of the Muscogee (Creek) community signs the Treaty of Indian Springs. The treaty forces the Muscogee (Creek) people to give up their lands east of the Chattahoochee River. The land becomes part of Georgia and Alabama.

1827

JULY

The Cherokee people write a **constitution** for their **nation**.

1828

NOVEMBER

Andrew Jackson is elected US president. Gold is found in Georgia on Cherokee land. Within months, thousands of white settlers invade Cherokee land to search for gold. A Georgia militia arrests any Cherokee people who join the search.

1830

MAY 28

The Indian Removal Act is passed in the US **House of Representatives** by just four votes. The bill states that all southern Indigenous peoples—Cherokee, Chickasaw, Choctaw, Muscogee (Creek), and Seminole—will be removed from their homes and forced west of the Mississippi River.

1832

MARCH 3

Chief Justice John Marshall delivers his opinion in the case of *Worcester v. Georgia*. Marshall says the state of Georgia has no right to enter Cherokee land. President Jackson ignores the decision.

MAY 9

Seminole leaders sign a treaty at Payne's Landing with James Gadsden, the US commissioner. The treaty agrees to relocation.

OCTOBER

Georgia holds a lottery. Winners get Cherokee land. If Cherokee landowners do not leave when asked, the militia moves them by force.

1835

DECEMBER 29

A small group of Cherokee leaders sign the Treaty of New Echota. They agree to give land west of the Mississippi River to the US government for $5 million. They **violate** Cherokee law when they sign the treaty.

1836

JANUARY

The Cherokee community refuses to accept the Treaty of New Echota.

1838

MAY

More than 6,000 militia troops invade Cherokee **territory**. They capture 19,000 Cherokee people and force them to temporary camps. Then, they move them to unsettled lands west of the Arkansas territory.

1839

MARCH

Indigenous people who have survived the Trail of Tears arrive in the West.

Key People
WHO'S WHO

The Trail of Tears affected tens of thousands of Indigenous individuals as they were forcibly relocated to unsettled lands west of the Mississippi River. Here are some of the key people involved.

Indigenous leaders

Osceola

John Ross

The Cherokee chief who took the **petition** refusing to accept the Treaty of New Echota to Washington, DC. He served as principal chief of the Cherokee people from 1828 to 1866, making him the longest-serving chief in Cherokee history.

Chief William McIntosh

A Muscogee (Creek) leader. He signed treaties with the US to try to keep peace.

Sequoyah

The inventor of the written alphabet used by the Cherokee people.

Levi Colbert

A Chickasaw leader. He wrote a letter to President Jackson expressing the Chickasaw people's frustration with General Coffee over the Treaty of Pontotoc Creek.

Chief Mushulatubbee

One of the most **influential** Choctaw chiefs. He **negotiated** several treaties, including the Treaty of Dancing Rabbit Creek. He supported removal but believed in upholding Choctaw traditions.

Osceola

A Seminole warrior who was unfairly captured by the US Army in 1837 when he came to a peaceful meeting under a **flag of truce**.

Those who favored removal

President Andrew Jackson

The seventh president of the US. During his time as a general, Jackson forced Indigenous peoples into signing treaties and giving up their land and rights. As president, he convinced **Congress** to write the Indian Removal Act, which he signed into law.

President Martin Van Buren

The eighth president of the US. He supported further removals of Indigenous peoples.

Major General Winfield Scott

Major General Winfield Scott

An American military leader. He was ordered to push out the Cherokee people living in Georgia, Alabama, North Carolina, and Tennessee after the Treaty of New Echota was **ratified**. His 3,000 troops, state militia, and volunteers used **inhumane** methods to move the Cherokee people to what settlers referred to as the **Indian Territory**.

The opposition

Elizur Butler

A **missionary** who condemned the Indian Removal Act and traveled with the Cherokee people, acting as their doctor.

Davy Crockett

Davy Crockett

A famous **frontiersman** and Tennessee congressman. He opposed the Indian Removal Act.

Ralph Waldo Emerson

A writer and **philosopher**. He wrote a letter to President Van Buren that criticized the US government for removing Indigenous people from their homelands.

Catharine Beecher

A teacher, writer, and educator who opposed the Indian Removal Act and encouraged women to petition Congress to vote against the legislation.

Chief Justice Marshall

A Supreme Court justice. He ruled that Indigenous peoples were **sovereign** and did not need to follow state laws.

Key Location FORT GIBSON

Fort Gibson was built in 1824 in what is now called Oklahoma. The US Army used it as a military post. It was one of several forts set up to keep peace on the western **frontier** and protect the border of the Louisiana Purchase. Fort Gibson's location made it a good starting point for military trips to explore the West.

This picture shows the commanding officer's quarters at Fort Gibson.

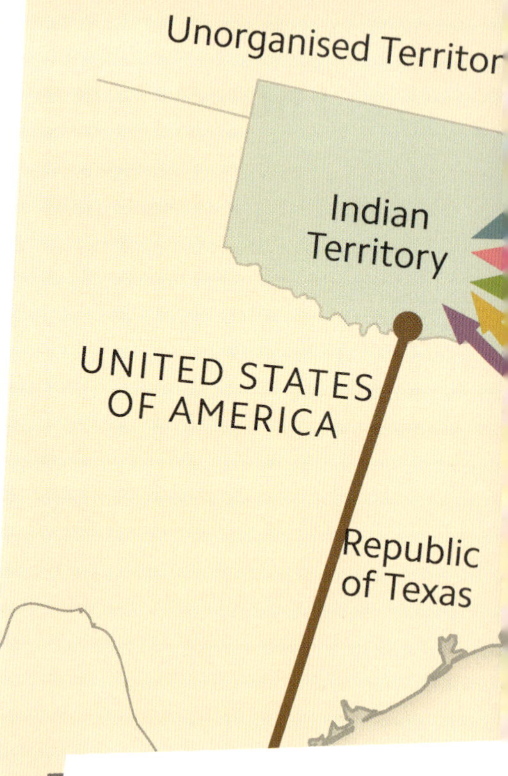

Fort Gibson was on the edge of the new land where the Indigenous people were forced to go.

FORCED RELOCATION

Thousands of people from the Cherokee, Muscogee (Creek), Seminole, Chickasaw, and Choctaw communities were moved west because of the Indian Removal Act of 1830. Many ended up passing through or near Fort Gibson after being forced to leave their homes.

This portrait portrays a Choctaw woman at Fort Gibson in 1834.

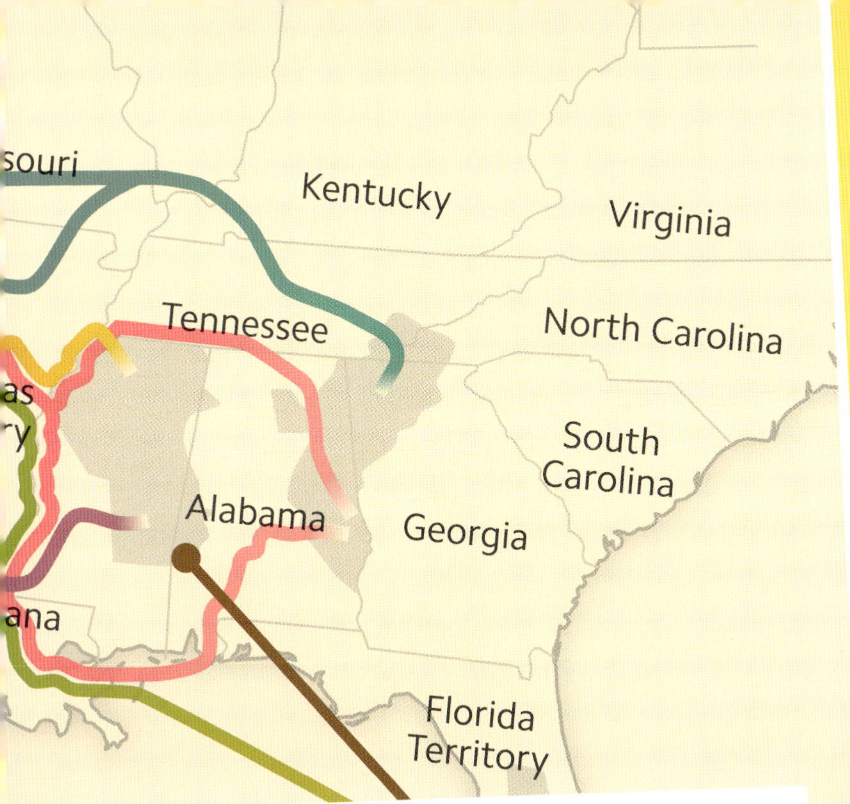

This map displays the different paths taken when Indigenous peoples were forced to move west. The arrows point in the direction in which they traveled. Each color indicates the direction of travel for different groups. The blue shows the route for the Cherokee people, pink for the Muscogee (Creek) people, yellow for the Chickasaw people, green for the Seminole people, and purple for the Choctaw people.

AN IMPORTANT CENTER

After the Indian Removal Act, Fort Gibson was used as a center for moving Indigenous communities to new areas. Back then, these areas were in what was called the Indian Territory. Now, it is known as Oklahoma.

The US government used the fort to negotiate and sign treaties with Indigenous peoples. The fort was also used for **administration**, such as deciding where people would live.

FORT GIBSON TODAY

Fort Gibson is managed by the Oklahoma Historical Society and is a National Historic Landmark.

A Closer Look at Indigenous Life

The beliefs and traditions of Indigenous communities have changed since the 1800s, but many of their core values are the same and remain important today.

Think about it

Indigenous people have always respected the natural environment. How could we make the world better by doing the same?

Indigenous peoples have always cared for nature. They try to take only what they need from the land.

The Seminole people made chickees. These houses had a raised floor, a roof made of palm leaves, and open sides.

LAND

Protecting and caring for the natural land is very important to Indigenous groups. Land is often communal. Traditionally, Indigenous peoples used it to hunt and farm, as well as grow crops such as tobacco, squash, corn, and beans.

HOMES

Southeastern Indigenous peoples built different types of homes that suited their environment and way of life. They used natural resources to construct buildings, such as logs held together with mud, wood coated with clay, and buffalo hides. Some peoples lived in log cabins or homes made with bricks and boards. Homes were often built around small villages.

This painting shows a Choctaw man wearing clothing that mixes Choctaw and European styles.

The Cherokee people used a special wooden buffalo mask in their forest buffalo dance. This dance was very important. It showed respect for buffalo and helped the community get ready for hunting.

CLOTHING

Each community had their own style of dress. The five southeastern peoples integrated European-American style by wearing shirts, pants, hats, and dresses. Other Indigenous groups remained unique in their clothing and **accessories**.

TRADITIONS AND BELIEFS

In the past, respect for nature and living in harmony with the land went hand-in-hand. Indigenous peoples celebrated their culture through storytelling and dance. **Elders** were very special in Indigenous communities. They had a great deal of knowledge about their community's history, traditions, and spiritual beliefs. Today, the value of respecting nature remains important. Storytelling and dance continue to play a big role in preserving and sharing Indigenous heritage. The wisdom of elders remains highly valued.

LANGUAGES

Southeastern Indigenous peoples spoke many different languages. The biggest group was called Muskogean. It included languages such as Choctaw, Creek, and Seminole. Choctaw was spoken in Alabama and Mississippi. Creek and Seminole were used in Georgia, Alabama, and Florida.

GOVERNANCE

The Indigenous communities formed their own governments, and some published written constitutions. Their governments were based on Indigenous leadership traditions.

A Closer Look at Settler Life

In the 1800s, many white settlers wanted to move west to find new places to live and work. But Indigenous peoples already called these areas home. Some Indigenous communities tried to live like the settlers. They farmed and dressed like them, and hoped this would let them keep their land. However, the settlers still wanted more. They asked the US government to move the Indigenous people away. The settlers sent letters and petitions to help make this happen.

LAND

White settlers valued individual property rights and private land ownership. Many settlers were farmers, ranchers, and wealthy **plantation** owners who grew crops such as cotton, tobacco, and sugar. Many **enslaved** people were forced to work on these plantations.

HOMES

When settlers moved to new places, they built different kinds of homes. The first homes were small and basic, like log cabins. These provided shelter and a place to sleep.

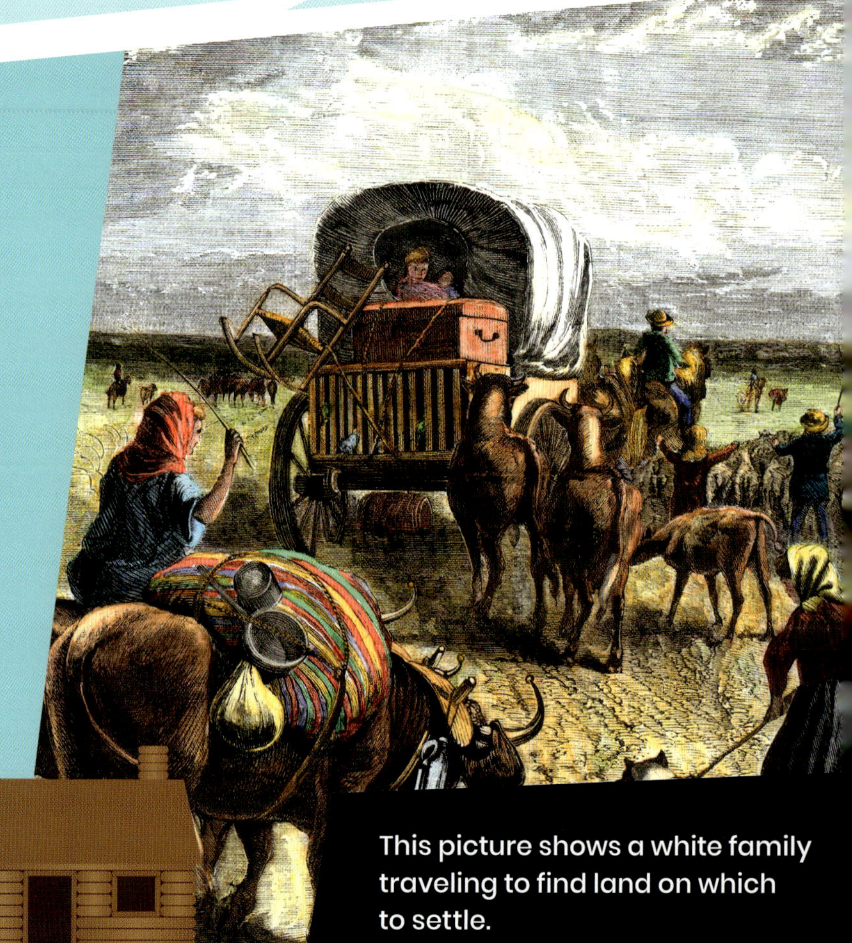

This picture shows a white family traveling to find land on which to settle.

CLOTHING

When they were not working, men wore pants, shirts, and hats, or suits. Women wore dresses, accessories, and hats to church and for special occasions.

TRADITIONS AND BELIEFS

Settlers had European, and often Christian, religious and cultural practices. Wealthy families had servants or enslaved people to do housework. Children attended school and went to Sunday school.

Think about it

How did white settlers and Indigenous people think differently about owning and using land?

LANGUAGES

White settlers mainly spoke English. Other languages were also spoken as more people came to the US. They brought languages like Italian and Yiddish. Over time, it became expected that everyone would learn and use English.

GOVERNANCE

By the 1800s, the US had a **democratic** political system, which was different from the **monarchies** who ruled in Europe. The US Constitution was written in 1787. As the country grew bigger, the government made new areas into territories. Later, these territories became states.

As settlers worked on their farms, they built stronger houses. These new homes had large kitchens and porches. They were good for farm life. Eventually, the settlements became towns.

Communities Under Threat

As more settlers arrived in the US, the Indigenous way of life started to change. White settlers often expected Indigenous people to be just like them, giving up their lifestyles, traditions, and languages. This clash of cultures led to significant challenges for Indigenous communities, including loss of land, exposure to new diseases, and the pressure to **assimilate**.

This painting depicts white settlers rushing to claim Indigenous land.

This picture shows Christian missionaries speaking to a group of Indigenous people. Indigenous communities were expected to abandon their traditions and religions, and follow Christianity.

LOSS OF LAND

Indigenous communities lived on their land for thousands of years before the arrival of Europeans. However, in the 1800s, they started to lose their land rapidly. In 1803, the US bought a huge amount of land from France. This is known as the Louisiana Purchase.

This picture shows the French leader Napoleon Bonaparte signing the Louisiana Purchase. The deal doubled the size of the US. The new land was west of the Mississippi River and added a lot of space to the country.

TREATIES

From 1814 to 1824, the US government made Indigenous peoples sign many treaties. But signing was not a free choice. Settlers wanted more land, and Indigenous communities feared attacks if they did not agree. These treaties took away many of their land rights. They lost most of their land in a short time.

DISEASES

Settlers brought new diseases, such as smallpox and measles, which were very dangerous for Indigenous communities. These diseases made many Indigenous people very sick because their bodies had never experienced them before.

Think about it

How might the rapid loss of land and exposure to deadly diseases have affected Indigenous people's cultures and ways of life?

EDUCATION

The US government made Indigenous children go to schools to teach them how to be more like white American people. The children were punished for speaking their own languages.

HUNTING

As settlers moved west and Indigenous communities lost their homelands, many Indigenous people had to stop hunting. For those who still did, tools such as guns changed how they hunted and fought.

The Indian Removal Act

The Indian Removal Act was signed by President Jackson on May 28, 1830. The new law allowed the government to move Indigenous communities from their homes in the southeastern US to regions west of the Mississippi River.

Think about it

The Indian Removal Act only passed in the House of Representatives by four votes. What does this tell us?

This is a picture of the Indian Removal Act. It passed in the House of Representatives by 101 votes in favor to 97 votes against.

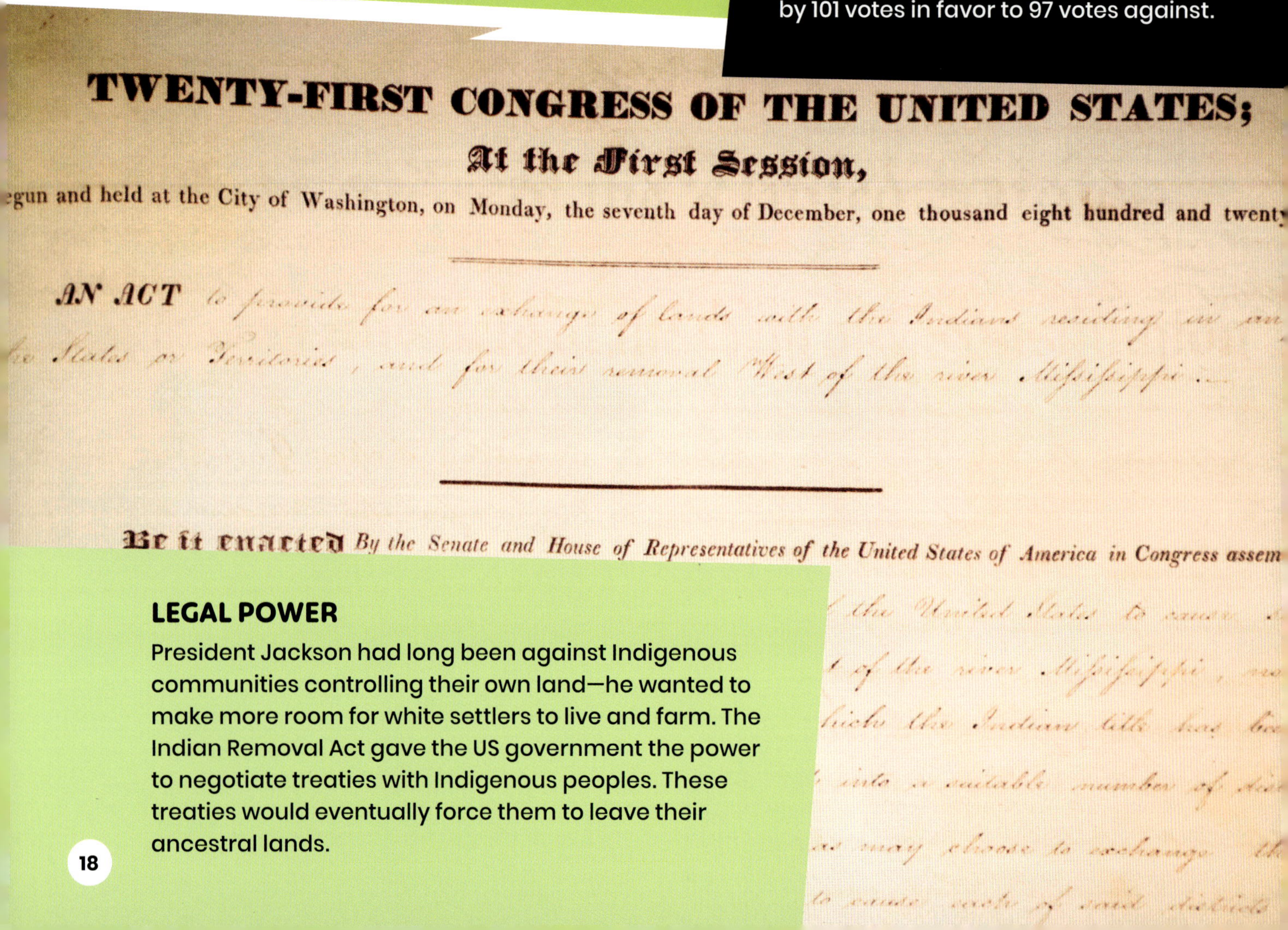

TWENTY-FIRST CONGRESS OF THE UNITED STATES;

At the First Session,

egun and held at the City of Washington, on Monday, the seventh day of December, one thousand eight hundred and twenty

AN ACT to provide for an exchange of lands with the Indians residing in an
he States or Territories, and for their removal West of the river Mississippi.

Be it enacted By the Senate and House of Representatives of the United States of America in Congress assem

LEGAL POWER

President Jackson had long been against Indigenous communities controlling their own land—he wanted to make more room for white settlers to live and farm. The Indian Removal Act gave the US government the power to negotiate treaties with Indigenous peoples. These treaties would eventually force them to leave their ancestral lands.

JUSTIFYING THE ACT

President Jackson told Congress that moving Indigenous peoples would make the frontier stronger and help the southeastern states grow faster. He presented the policy as **benevolent** and **beneficial** to both the US and Indigenous communities. The government promised the communities money, food, and help if they gave up their land. But many people did not want to leave their homes.

President Jackson's speech in support of the Indian Removal Act did not tell the whole truth about his motivations for moving Indigenous peoples. He also did not talk about how much it would hurt the communities.

President Jackson negotiated 9 out of 11 treaties that took away land from Indigenous peoples.

The forced removal of Indigenous peoples meant they had to take all their belongings and settle on unfamiliar land.

The Act Opposed

Many American people did not support the Indian Removal Act. When it was first proposed in 1829, groups of citizens from all over the US sent letters to the government saying it was wrong. The Cherokee Nation went to court twice to protect their rights.

CONSTITUTION
OF THE
CHEROKEE NATION,
MADE AND ESTABLISHED
AT A
GENERAL CONVENTION OF DELEGATES,
DULY AUTHORISED FOR THAT PURPOSE,
AT
NEW ECHOTA,
JULY 26, 1827.

In 1827, the Cherokee leaders wrote their first constitution. They hoped it would protect their right to stay on their land and govern themselves.

CHEROKEE NATION V. GEORGIA

In 1828, the Cherokee Nation asked the Supreme Court to stop the state of Georgia from enforcing laws that took rights away from their people, forcing them from their land. Led by John Ross, the Cherokee chief, the Cherokee Nation claimed that the US had violated signed treaties. But in 1831, the Supreme Court said it could not help because the Cherokee Nation was not a foreign country.

Even though they lost the case, Chief John Ross led the Cherokee people to resist removal from their land. His work resulted in another important Supreme Court case, *Worcester v. Georgia*, in 1832.

WORCESTER V. GEORGIA

In the early 1830s, a group of white missionaries, including Samuel Worcester, lived on Cherokee land in Georgia. In 1830, Georgia passed a law that stated that "white persons" could not live on Cherokee land unless they got a license from the governor. They also had to swear loyalty to Georgia. The missionaries helped convince the Cherokee people not to follow Georgia's state laws. Authorities in Georgia arrested Worcester. His arrest led to a legal case that went all the way to the US Supreme Court, known as *Worcester v. Georgia.*

The Supreme Court ruled that Georgia had no right to make laws in Cherokee territory, especially since the Cherokee Nation had signed treaties with the US government.

Ralph Waldo Emerson was a famous writer and philosopher who spoke out against forcing Indigenous people off their land. In the 1830s, he gave speeches at public meetings to protest the Indian Removal Act and wrote to the government to argue against the policy.

SPEAKING OUT

Activists such as Catharine Beecher, Ralph Waldo Emerson, Jeremiah Evarts, Davy Crockett, and many others did what they could to let other American people know that the forced removal of Indigenous communities was cruel and **unethical**.

Jeremiah Evarts

Think about it

Why is it important to learn about people who opposed unjust laws in the past?

Cherokee Nation Against Georgia

It is important to remember that Cherokee people communicated in Cherokee.

Chief John Ross
Principal chief of the Cherokee Nation

Elias Boudinot
Editor of the *Cherokee Phoenix*

William Wirt
Attorney representing the Cherokee Nation in the Supreme Court

Justice John Marshall
Chief justice of the Supreme Court

Justice Smith Thompson
A Supreme Court justice and supporter of the Cherokee Nation

In 1825, the Cherokee Nation established New Echota as their national capital.

This is our home! We are proud to be Cherokee!

Yes, our ancestors have lived on this land for generations.

The town square was a hub of activity and community spirit. The Council House was used for important meetings.

In 1827, the Cherokee Nation formed their own constitution. It aimed to protect Cherokee land and the people's rights.
CONSTITUTION OF THE CHEROKEE NATION
MADE AND ESTABLISHED AT A GENERAL CONVENTION OF DELEGATES
DULY AUTHORISED FOR THAT PURPOSE AT
NEW ECHOTA, JULY 26, 1827.
With this constitution, we declare our sovereignty!
We are a nation, governed by our own laws.
We must do all we can to defend our land!
With this constitution, we can show the United States that we are equals.

The *Cherokee Phoenix*, published in Cherokee and English, fought against Georgia's land encroachment.
Every issue we publish is a sign of our determination.
The newspaper shared the stories and voices of the Cherokee people.
I fear Georgia will continue to encroach on our land.
This outlines Georgia's recent actions and how we can defend our territory.
With every edition, we strengthen our voice!

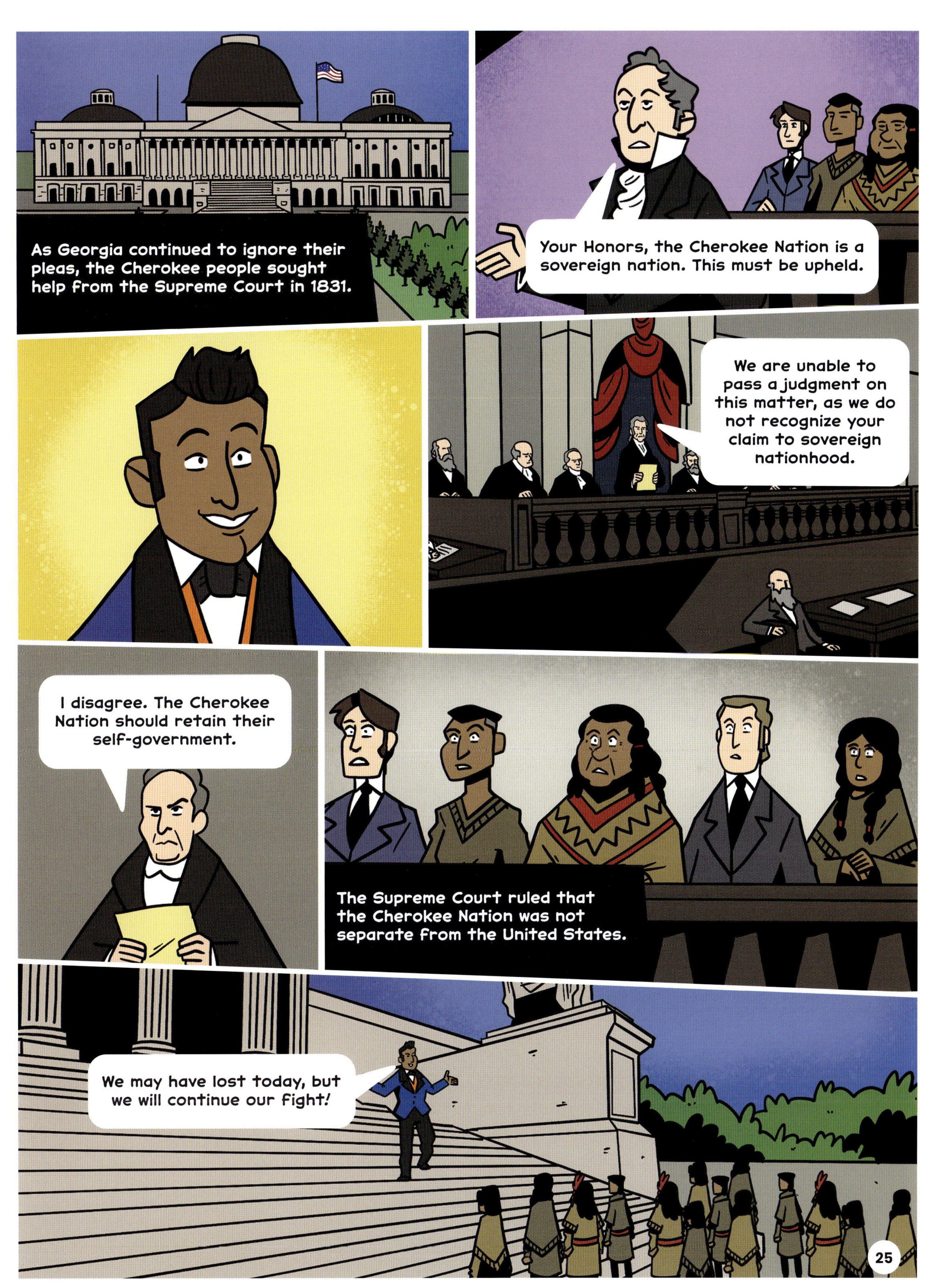
As Georgia continued to ignore their pleas, the Cherokee people sought help from the Supreme Court in 1831.
Your Honors, the Cherokee Nation is a sovereign nation. This must be upheld.
We are unable to pass a judgment on this matter, as we do not recognize your claim to sovereign nationhood.
I disagree. The Cherokee Nation should retain their self-government.
The Supreme Court ruled that the Cherokee Nation was not separate from the United States.
We may have lost today, but we will continue our fight!

The Removal of the Choctaw People

The Choctaw people lived in what is now central and southern Mississippi, parts of eastern Louisiana, and western Alabama. They were there for thousands of years before the arrival of European settlers. Their community was the first Indigenous group to be forcibly removed from their ancestral lands.

The Choctaw people were known for being excellent athletes and warriors.

LOSS OF LAND

From 1801 to 1830, the Choctaw people made several deals with the US government. The first treaty was signed on December 17, 1801, at Fort Adams, Mississippi. The Choctaw community gave up more than 4,000 sq miles (10,000 sq km) of land to the US. They got $2,000 worth of goods in return, including guns, food, and tobacco. This is about $1.4 million in today's money. Over the next 24 years, the Choctaw people made six more agreements with the US, losing around 25,000 sq miles (65,000 sq km) of their ancestral land.

Pushmataha was a key leader of the Choctaw people in the early 1800s. He fought hard for the rights and independence of his community.

This map from 1836 shows the land assigned to the Choctaw community west of the Mississippi, after the Indian Removal Act.

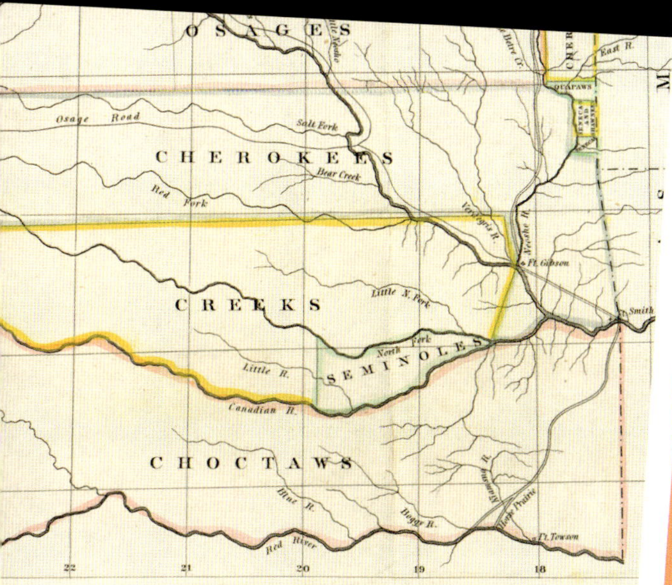

Fascinating fact

In 1847, the Choctaw people donated money to help the Irish people during the **potato famine**. In Ireland, there is a monument to **commemorate** this act of kindness.

THE TREATY OF DANCING RABBIT CREEK

White settlers wanted the Choctaw people to leave Mississippi and move west of the Mississippi River. The Treaty of Dancing Rabbit Creek was signed on September 27, 1830. The Choctaw community agreed to give up around 17,000 sq miles (44,000 sq km) of their land in Mississippi and Alabama. In return, they got new land in what is now Oklahoma.

THE JOURNEY

Between 1831 and 1833, about 13,000 Choctaw people moved to Oklahoma. About 4,000 Choctaw people refused to leave. Those who left took wagons, horses, and boats, while others walked. The journey was extremely difficult. For about 3,000 Choctaw individuals, it was **fatal**. People did not have enough food to eat. Many got very sick, suffered in harsh weather, and did not have suitable shelter.

IMPACT

The treatment by the US government, tough conditions of the new land, and loss of life devastated the Choctaw community. Today, there are three main groups of Choctaw people: the Choctaw Nation of Oklahoma, the Mississippi Band of Choctaw Indians, and the MOWA Band of Choctaw Indians in Alabama. The US government recognizes the first two groups, but not the MOWA Band. An Alabama congressman has tried four times to get them recognized, without success. About 80 percent of the MOWA Band lives in **poverty**.

REMEMBERING THEIR ANCESTORS

Bike rides and memorial walks are two ways Choctaw descendants remember what happened in their people's history.

The Removal of the Muscogee (Creek) People

Long ago, the ancestors of the Muscogee (Creek) community built big earth mounds. They were used for important things like homes for leaders and places for spiritual ceremonies. The Muscogee (Creek) group was not just one community, but many communities joined together. The Muscogee (Creek) people made their homes along rivers in what are now Alabama and Georgia. They were welcoming and let other groups join them. By 1775, they were very powerful in the South.

Red Eagle, a Muscogee (Creek) chief who fought for the Red Sticks, surrendered to General Andrew Jackson after the Creek War.

THE TREATY OF NEW YORK

In 1790, Muscogee (Creek) and US leaders signed the Treaty of New York. This agreement established peace between the two parties. It also showed where Muscogee (Creek) land ended, and where US land began.

THE CREEK WAR

From 1813 to 1814, the Muscogee (Creek) members fought a civil war. It was between two groups of Muscogee (Creek) people. The Lower Creek group fought against the more traditional Upper Creek group, also known as the Red Sticks. The Red Sticks were defeated at the Battle of Horseshoe Bend. After the war, the Muscogee (Creek) leaders signed the Treaty of Fort Jackson. It forced them to give up a lot of their land to the US.

THE TREATY OF INDIAN SPRINGS

In 1825, William McIntosh, a Muscogee (Creek) leader, secretly signed the Treaty of Indian Springs. This gave all Muscogee (Creek) land in Georgia and part of Alabama to the US. When the rest of the community found out, McIntosh was **executed**. In 1826, the new Treaty of Washington was negotiated but it did not restore Muscogee (Creek) lands.

FORCED REMOVAL

After the Indian Removal Act of 1830, the Muscogee (Creek) leaders signed the Treaty of Cusseta in 1832. They gave the rest of their land to the US. Some Muscogee (Creek) people chose to leave their homes on their own. But many others did not want to go. They had to deal with settlers who came onto their land and often used violence against them.

The Treaty of New York was the first significant agreement between an Indigenous group and the US after American Independence.

THE JOURNEY

When the Muscogee (Creek) people left, they did not have time to harvest their crops. They did not have clothing for the winter. About 23,000 Muscogee (Creek) individuals were removed. Some were forced to wear chains. It took about three months to travel 750 miles (1,200 km) by land and 400 miles (600 km) by water.

IMPACT

Individuals had to leave behind many things they owned. Even worse, they had to leave behind the graves of their ancestors. About 8,000 Muscogee (Creek) people died over 20 years as a direct result of the forced removal.

REMEMBERING THEIR ANCESTORS

Hickory Ground in Wetumpka, Alabama, is an important historic site for the Muscogee (Creek) community. Every March, people gather to remember those who fought at the Battle of Horseshoe Bend in 1814. They honor Muscogee (Creek) warriors and share their history.

Think about it

How do you think being forced to leave their homeland changed how the Muscogee (Creek) people felt about special places like Hickory Ground?

The Removal of the Cherokee People

Cherokee territory once spanned the areas now known as West Virginia, Virginia, Kentucky, Tennessee, North Carolina, South Carolina, Georgia, and Alabama. The Cherokee people lived there for thousands of years. When a Cherokee couple married, a husband joined his wife's **clan**. Men hunted while women grew crops and gathered food. Towns were independent. But treaties with Great Britain and the US ultimately reduced Cherokee land by 90 percent.

A WRITING SYSTEM

In 1809, a Cherokee chief called Sequoyah started developing a system for writing the Cherokee language called a **syllabary**. Up to this point, the Cherokee community had used an oral language.

Fascinating fact

The *Cherokee Phoenix* was the first newspaper in the US made by Indigenous people. It was printed in Cherokee and English and launched on February 21, 1828. It helped the Cherokee people talk about their rights and share their opinions.

The Cherokee people started using Sequoyah's syllabary in 1825. By 1830, almost 90 percent of the community could read and write in Cherokee.

The petition was taken to Washington, DC, by the Cherokee chief John Ross. But the petition was ignored.

THE TREATY OF NEW ECHOTA

The Treaty of New Echota was signed in 1835 by four community members who had no right to represent the Cherokee Nation. The treaty was rejected by the Cherokee people, but it was ratified in the US **Senate** by one vote. A petition protesting the treaty was circulated among the Cherokee community. It was hundreds of pages long and asked the US government to protect it from Georgia's unfair laws. It was signed by 90 percent of Cherokee people.

THE JOURNEY

On May 10, 1838, US soldiers began forcing the Cherokee people out of their homes. Those who did not want to leave were forced to go at gunpoint. Soldiers used their weapons to make the Cherokee people march from eastern Alabama to Montgomery, in the center of the state. There, they were kept in a fenced camp. Months later, those who survived followed the US military west. By 1839, about 16,000 Cherokee individuals made the journey to the so-called Indian Territory. More than 4,000 died.

IMPACT

In 1839, the Cherokee Nation wrote a new constitution. This helped bring them together after their long, hard journey to a new home. The new Cherokee capital became Tahlequah, Oklahoma. There, people built government buildings, businesses, homes, and schools. Despite this, the loss of their homeland and deaths of their ancestors are still felt today.

REMEMBERING THEIR ANCESTORS

A stone monument in Blythe Ferry, Tennessee, commemorates the names of ancestors. The descendants also maintain traditions including dance, beadwork, storytelling, and recipes.

This stone monument was put up in 2005.

The Removal of the Chickasaw People

The Chickasaw community lived in parts of what are now northern Mississippi, northwestern Alabama, western Tennessee, and southwestern Kentucky. They were skilled traders and fighters, organized into different clans. The Chickasaw people took pride in defending their land and keeping their culture strong.

The Chickasaw Warrior is a bronze sculpture by Seminole artist, Enoch Kelly Haney.

THE TREATY OF PONTOTOC CREEK

In 1832, the Chickasaw community had to give up over 23,000 sq miles (63,000 sq km) of land to the US government. This agreement was called the Treaty of Pontotoc Creek. The US promised to help the Chickasaw people move and give them food supplies for a year.

THE TREATY OF DOAKSVILLE

In 1837, the Chickasaw leaders made a deal with the Choctaw community. This was called the Treaty of Doaksville. The Choctaw people agreed that the Chickasaw people could live on their land in the Indian Territory, in what is now Oklahoma.

In the early 1700s, the Chickasaw community fought against the French. The Chickasaw people were allies of the British Army, while the French side had help from other Indigenous groups.

Convention between the
Choctaw & Chickasaw
Indians.
Concluded 17th Jany 1837.
Approved by Senate 25th

The Treaty of Doaksville was an important agreement between the Choctaw and Chickasaw nations.

THE JOURNEY

Though the Chickasaw community was forced to move, their removal was paid for. Unlike other Indigenous groups, they also decided the date of their move. But the food promised to them was rotten and the blankets they were given were bad quality. Almost 5,000 Chickasaw individuals traveled hundreds of miles in severe weather. It is estimated that 500 people died from diseases such as smallpox and dysentery.

Fascinating fact

The first recorded contact between the Chickasaw group and European people took place in 1540 when Spanish explorer Hernando de Soto met the community.

IMPACT

Plains Indian communities were already living on the land when the Chickasaw people arrived. They were surprised to see the Chickasaw members building homes and farms on land they had always used. This made them confused and angry, and led to fights between the two groups.

REMEMBERING THEIR ANCESTORS

Today, the Chickasaw people honor their past. In 1983, the Chickasaw Nation set up their own government again and wrote a new constitution. They work to keep their traditions alive and teach others about their history.

The Chickasaw people separated from the Choctaw community in 1856 to reclaim their independence. They wrote their own constitution. It was drafted by Chickasaw leader, Holmes Colbert, when he was just 26 years old.

The Removal of the Seminole People

The Seminole people have a long history in Florida, dating back thousands of years. The community **originates** from a combination of different Indigenous groups and people who escaped enslavement.

Billy Bowlegs was an important Seminole leader in Florida in the 1800s. He fought the US government to try to stop it from forcing the Seminole community to leave their land.

Fascinating fact

The Seminole community is the only Indigenous group to have never signed a peace treaty with the US government after war.

BLACK SEMINOLE INDIVIDUALS

Enslaved Black American people who escaped rice plantations in South Carolina and Georgia joined the Seminole group. These **fugitives** became known as Black Seminole people, helping the Seminole community with **tropical agriculture** and fighting in wars against white settlers.

FIRST SEMINOLE WAR

General Andrew Jackson attacked the Seminole people in 1817. He saw them as a threat to Georgia.

This picture depicts Seminole chiefs being captured by American soldiers.

TERRITORIAL FLORIDA

With the signing of the Transcontinental Treaty in 1819, Spain gave up all claims to East and West Florida. Florida was now a US territory. Andrew Jackson became the governor of the new **province**, a position he held for 11 weeks.

THE TREATY OF PAYNE'S LANDING

In 1832, the Seminole leaders agreed to give up their land in Florida and move west. They got $15,400 (about $4.4 million in today's money), clothes, and blankets in return.

SECOND SEMINOLE WAR

In 1835, the US Army came to forcibly remove the Seminole community. But they did not want to leave. For seven years, about 3,000 Seminole warriors fought against 30,000 US soldiers. Known as the Second Seminole War, it cost the US more than $20 million, about $5.2 billion in today's money.

THIRD SEMINOLE WAR

The Third Seminole War lasted from 1855 to 1858. It started when US Army workers destroyed a Seminole farm. Billy Bowlegs led the Seminole community in fighting against US soldiers.

THE JOURNEY

Around 4,000 Seminole people ended up leaving Florida after the war. They were taken to local towns like Tampa Bay and then ferried across the Gulf of Mexico to New Orleans, Louisiana. Some Seminole individuals died along the way, while others were very unwell when they arrived in the Indian Territory. Fewer than 500 Seminole people remained in Florida.

IMPACT

By the end of the Third Seminole War in 1858, there were only about 200 Seminole people left in their ancestral lands. In the West, the Seminole people had to share land and obey Muscogee (Creek) laws. They established an independent Seminole Nation in 1856.

REMEMBERING THEIR ANCESTORS

One way that Seminole descendants remember their history is through names. In Oklahoma, people were given names that translate in English to phrases such as "people going" and "looking back."

In Florida, some Seminole people still live in traditional houses called chickees.

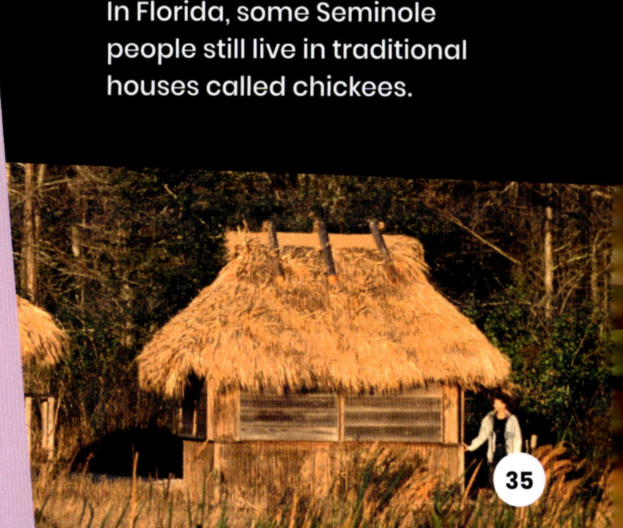

Lessons from History

An estimated 60,000 Indigenous individuals were forcibly removed from their homelands. This tragic event teaches important lessons about respecting the rights of all people and keeping cultures alive. So why do we remember the Trail of Tears and what can we learn from it?

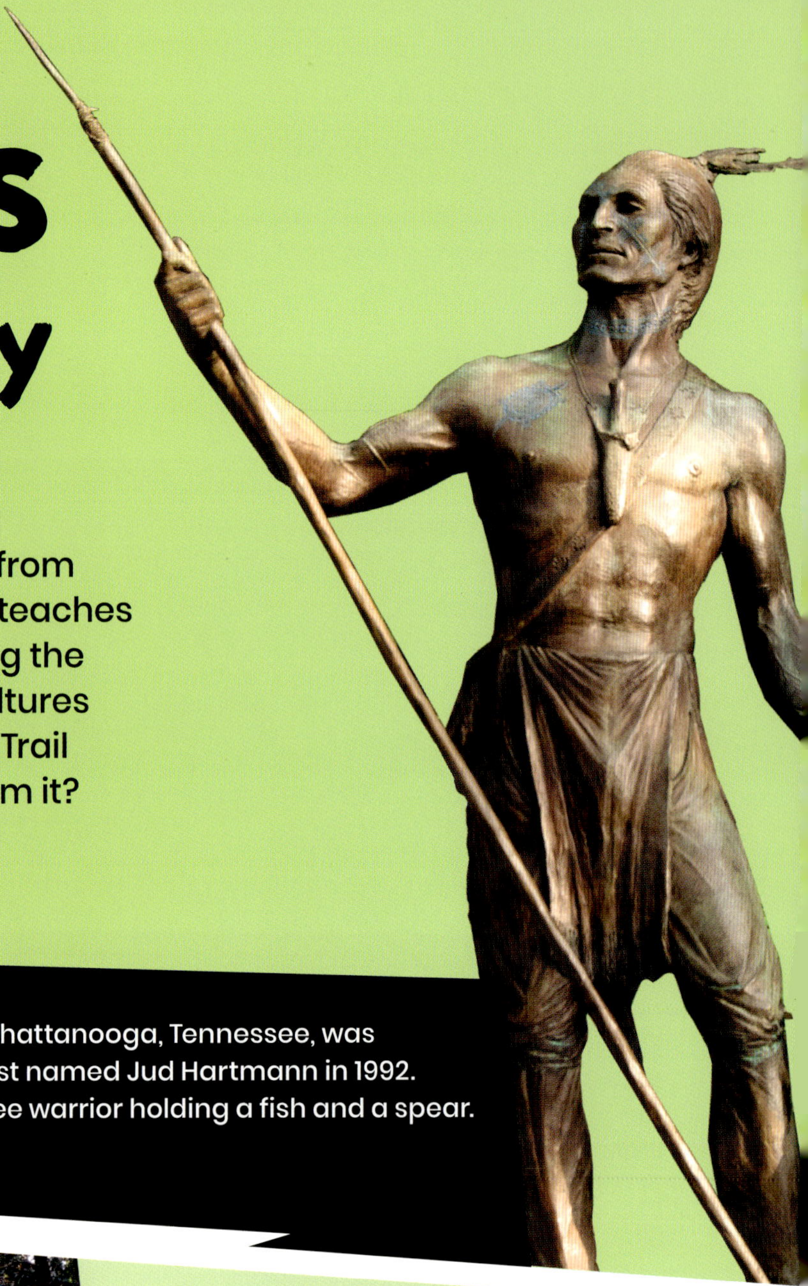

This sculpture in Chattanooga, Tennessee, was created by an artist named Jud Hartmann in 1992. It shows a Cherokee warrior holding a fish and a spear.

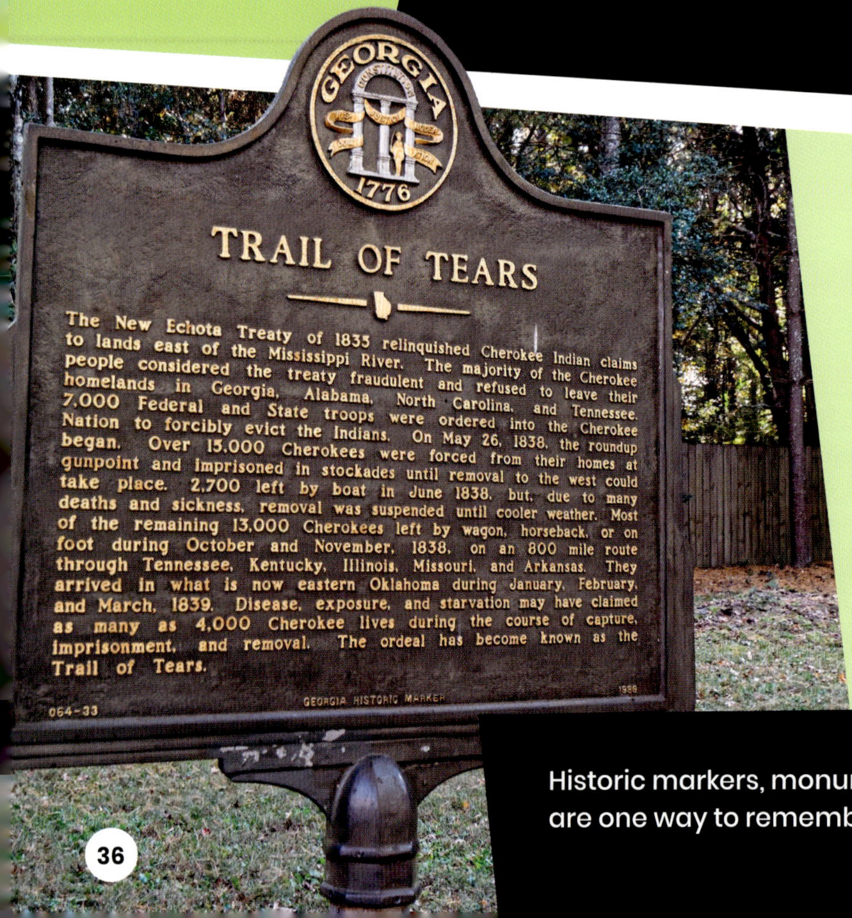

PRESERVING HISTORIC MEMORY

In 1987, US Congress named the Trail of Tears a National Historic Trail. But in 2009, the trail more than doubled in size. This is because new records showed that there were more roundup sites, separation locations, and routes than originally thought. The National Historic Trail now commemorates the memory of those who suffered forced removal, as well as those who died on the journey.

Historic markers, monuments, and trails are one way to remember the Trail of Tears.

The National Museum of the American Indian provides a place for Indigenous people to share their history, art, and traditions more widely.

ACKNOWLEDGING PAST WRONGS

The US government's Land Buy-Back Program ran from 2012 to 2022. It tried to address some of the historic injustices experienced by Indigenous communities. The program gave land back to Indigenous nations and also paid money to individuals. It was a small step toward apologizing and making up for past mistakes.

CELEBRATING INDIGENOUS CULTURES

Museums and centers such as the National Museum of the American Indian, established by Congress in 1989, preserve and celebrate Indigenous cultures.

Deb Haaland is the first Indigenous person to serve as a US cabinet secretary. She knows how Indigenous communities are still impacted by the events of the Trail of Tears today. Understanding these challenges can help create a fairer future for everyone.

REMEMBRANCE DAY

The Trail of Tears Remembrance Day is held each year on September 16. This day helps us remember the suffering and injustice experienced by Indigenous people. It reminds us how important it is to appreciate all cultures.

Uncovering the Truth
Primary Sources

A lot is known about the people and events of the Trail of Tears. This is because there are so many primary sources still available to historians today. A primary source is a document or object created at the time of a historical event.

Primary sources include

- official documents
- letters
- diaries
- paintings or drawings
- photographs
- sound recordings
- videos

Photo of original source

For the Rale
A letter from the Cherokee chiefs
Excellency, Gov. Jos. McMinn in answer
certain communications of his respecting the
and removal to the west.
In Council near Cherokee
Friend and Brother, Agency November 1818.
Your communication of
the 10th inst. was this day read in open council,
explained and interpreted to the chiefs assembled
after deliberating with that attention which
its contents justly merited, we have prepared
the following sentiments from the centre of
our hearts, and though expressed through the
organs of unrefined sense, in all the simplicity
of nature, incapable of polishing words, you
will at once see the sentiments of your red
brothers, in their true colours.
Brother, we know that we are under the protection
of the government of the United States, therefore
we are not insensible that we are also dependent
on the humanity, generosity, and friendship
of that magnanimous Government

DIFFERENT POINTS OF VIEW

Primary and secondary sources may tell different stories depending on the views of the people who created them. An Indigenous person forced from their land would have a different perspective than a settler who wanted to move west. It is important to question sources—doing this helps us to understand them and understand different perspectives better.

A LETTER FROM THE CHEROKEE CHIEFS

This is an extract from a letter written in 1818. It is from the Cherokee chiefs to Joseph McMinn, the governor of Tennessee. It is a response to Governor McMinn's thoughts about Cherokee land and the idea of settlers moving west.

Modern-day text

November 21, 1818

Friend and Brother,

Your message of the 18th was read, explained, and interpreted to all the chiefs in council today.

We have carefully considered its contents and prepared this response with sincerity. Though our words may not be refined, we hope you will see our true feelings.

Brother, we know we are under the protection of the US government and depend on its humanity, generosity, and friendship. We are committed to honoring all our obligations to the US [...]

[...] Brother, we agree that the Great Spirit supports leaders who seek the best for their people.

With respect, we ask you: would it be fair to force an entire nation to leave their homeland against their will? They would have to abandon the land where their ancestors are buried. They would lose the support promised to them by a treaty approved by the US government. In return, they would only get a small payment that does not even cover the cost of moving.

The Cherokee leaders got Governor McMinn's message. They discussed it at a meeting.

The Cherokee leaders read McMinn's message very carefully. They are writing back to share their honest thoughts.

They will do everything the US expects of them, according to official treaties and agreements.

They both believe in a higher power. By saying this, the Cherokee leaders are finding common ground with McMinn.

The chiefs say it is unfair to force them from their ancestral land. It breaks promises and the payment the government is offering is not enough.

Look at the letter, then read the modernized version of the text and answer the questions below.

Quick questions

- On what date was this letter written?
- What do the Cherokee leaders and Governor McMinn agree on?
- What does the greeting "friend and brother" show about their relationship?

Discussion questions

- What do you think the Cherokee leaders hoped to achieve by writing this letter?
- Why do the Cherokee leaders ask Governor McMinn a question at the end?
- What does this letter suggest about the relationship between the Cherokee leaders and the US government in 1818?

- The letter was written on November 21, 1818.
- They agreed that a higher power supports leaders who seek the best for their people.
- The greeting shows a respectful approach by the Cherokee leaders.

Uncovering the Truth

Secondary Sources

A secondary source is a document or object created after the event, or by someone who was not directly involved in the event. Secondary sources can explain or interpret primary sources. They help in understanding an event.

Secondary sources include

- news articles
- books
- media documentaries
- encyclopedias

AN IRISH MONUMENT

From 1845 to 1852, Ireland was struck by the potato famine. Potatoes were Ireland's main food, and there were not enough to feed everyone. As a result, many Irish people went hungry and suffered. The Choctaw community felt sorry for them—they had also suffered greatly when they were forced to move from their land. The Choctaw people decided to donate $170 to help those starving in Ireland. In today's money, their gift would be worth more than $6,000. This shows how much the Choctaw people cared about helping the Irish people during an extremely difficult time.

To help remember this kind act, an Irish artist named Alex Pentek designed and created a monument called *Kindred Spirits*. It is made of stainless steel and took a year to create.

It is estimated that around one million people died as a result of the potato famine in Ireland.

The *Kindred Spirits* monument was unveiled in 2015 in a park in County Cork, Ireland, for everyone to see.

The sculpture has nine eagle feathers. Eagle feathers are considered **sacred** by the Choctaw people.

The feathers are 20 ft (6.1 m) tall. Each one is different.

The sculpture is in a park where everyone can see it.

The feathers stand in a circle. They form the shape of a bowl.

Look at the sculpture, then read the annotations and answer the questions below.

Quick questions

- What is the name of the sculpture? What does it mean?
- When and where was it shared with the public?
- Why do you think the sculpture is in the shape of a bowl?

Discussion questions

- Why do you think the artist chose to make a sculpture showing eagle feathers?
- What do you think influenced the Choctaw people's decision to help those in need in Ireland?
- What does this story show about relationships between people from different geographic and cultural backgrounds?

- The sculpture is called *Kindred Spirits*. This means people who are very similar in how they think and feel.
- It was unveiled in 2015 in a park in County Cork, Ireland.
- The bowl shape might symbolize offering or giving, representing the Choctaw Nation's generous donation to the Irish people during the potato famine.

Vocabulary Builder
Forced to Move

How might a newspaper report the events of the Trail of Tears? Read this fictional article about the forced removal of Indigenous people. Pay attention to key words that describe how people are reacting and how they feel.

PRESIDENT'S GREED MOVES PEOPLE WEST

President Andrew Jackson continues to follow up on his Indian Removal Act of 1830 and remove Indigenous communities in the Southeast. His desire to rule over more land has been **bolstered** by the discovery of gold in Georgia. More and more white settlers are calling on the president to move Indigenous peoples west.

Meanwhile, various organizations continue to sign and send petitions to Washington, DC, in protest. Individuals such as Ms Catharine Beecher and Mr Davy Crockett are also being vocal about the forced removal.

In addition, Mr William Penn has been writing articles in the newspaper about this **calamity**.

The Choctaw community was the first to be moved, followed by the Muscogee (Creek) group. The Cherokee people tried to beat President Jackson in court. They were defeated the first time and ignored by the president himself when they succeeded the second time. The Chickasaw people then found themselves in the same **plight**. Now the Seminole community are battling their second war to avoid the move.

Imagine you are reporting on the events of the Trail of Tears for a newspaper. Then use the article on page 42 and the prompts and word bank below to write your own news story.

- **What is happening?**
- **How are people feeling?**
- **What details can you add to inform readers?**

Removal	ancestral lands, forced march, negotiation, petition, relocation, Removal Act, reservation, resettlement, resistance, treaty
Reactions	anguish, betrayal, despair, frustration, grief, injustice, outrage, powerlessness, resentment, sadness, sorrow, trauma
Descriptions	brutal, dangerous, destructive, devastating, disruptive, harsh, grueling, inhumane, tragic, violent

Glossary

Accessory An item someone wears or carries to enhance their clothing or appearance.

Administration The processes and procedures that an organization carries out to help it run smoothly.

Agriculture The practice of working the soil and producing crops, also called farming.

Ancestral Something related to one's ancestors.

Assimilate To absorb one culture into another.

Atrocity A terrible, shocking act or situation.

Beneficial Helpful, good.

Benevolent Kind, good.

Bolstered To be supported.

Calamity A great misfortune or misery.

Civilized To have just laws and good standards of behavior.

Clan A family group.

Commemorate To memorialize or otherwise remember something historic.

Communal Something shared by people in a community.

Congress A body of government in the US charged with discussing ideas and making decisions. It is made up of the Senate and the House of Representatives.

Constitution The written laws that govern a country. The United States has separate constitutions for each state, in addition to the United States Constitution that applies to the entire country. Many countries have constitutions.

Democratic When people have the power to choose their leaders and to participate in decision-making through voting.

Elder An older member of a community, often respected for their wisdom.

Enslaved To be forced to work for someone else without the freedom to stop or leave.

Executed To be put to death as punishment for a crime.

Fatal Deadly, lethal.

Flag of truce A peaceful meeting with an enemy to have a discussion.

Frontier An area of land that is beyond what a society considers as settled.

Frontiersman A person who lives or travels in an undeveloped area, often one that is newly settled.

Fugitive Someone who is running away or hiding from the law.

House of Representatives One of the two chambers of Congress that makes and passes federal laws. It has 435 representatives who can cast votes.

Indian Territory From 1834 to 1907, the vast region of the West that is now the state of Oklahoma and parts of Kansas, Nebraska, Missouri, Colorado, North Dakota, South Dakota, Montana, and Wyoming.

Indigenous Indigenous peoples are groups of people who are the original inhabitants of a region or area. There may be many different groups of Indigenous peoples within a region, each with their own languages and cultures.

Inferior Of lower importance, value, or rank.

Influential To have the ability to affect something else.

Inhumane Without kindness or mercy.

Legislation Laws made by a legislative body, such as Congress.

Militia A group of citizens with some military training who are called to assist the army in an emergency.

Missionary Someone who travels and preaches from place to place, trying to convert people to their religion.

Monarchy A form of government that has a single person known as a monarch at its head. Monarchs use titles such as king, queen, emperor, or empress.

Nation Used to refer to the governing bodies of some Indigenous communities, such as the Cherokee Nation, the Choctaw Nation, and so on.

Negotiated To come to an agreement following a discussion.

Originate To come from.

Petition A written request or demand for change, often including signatures of supporters.

Philosopher Someone who studies ideas in search of wisdom.

Plantation A large farm that grows crops to sell.

Plea An appeal or call for help.

Plight A difficult situation or condition.

Potato famine A period in Ireland from 1845 to 1852 in which a disease destroyed potato crops. About one million Irish people died from starvation. Millions more left the country.

Poverty The state of being poor; lacking money or possessions.

Prejudice An unfair opinion or feeling, especially one that is formed without much knowledge or understanding. It is often directed toward people because of their race, heritage, religion, sex, gender, or other characteristics.

Province A large area of land that has its own government.

Psychologically Relating to the mind.

Ratified To be approved or signed into law.

Sacred To be holy, or of great spiritual importance.

Senate The US Senate is the Upper House of Congress.

Sought Looked for, asked for, or requested.

Source A written document, artifact, or building that provides information relating to the past. Sources are also known as evidence.

Sovereign Something or someone that is politically independent.

Syllabary A writing system where each symbol represents a syllable.

Territory An area of land that is controlled by a particular group of people, country, or government.

Treaty An official agreement between two or more groups, such as two countries. It states how they will act or what they will do.

Tropical A hot and humid climate.

Unethical Morally or legally wrong.

Violate To go against or break, such as the law.

Index

Acknowledgments

The publisher would like to thank the following for their kind permission to reproduce their photographs:

(Key: a-above; b-below/bottom; c-centre; f-far; l-left; r-right; t-top)

4-5 Alamy Stock Photo: Album (b); Jim Zuckerman (t). **6 Alamy Stock Photo**: The Granger Collection (t); The Print Collector (b). **8 Alamy Stock Photo**: AAA Photostock (cr). **9 Alamy Stock Photo**: IanDagnall Computing (b); incamerastock (t). **10 Alamy Stock Photo**: Allen Creative, Steve Allen (bl). **10-11 Alamy Stock Photo**: SBS Eclectic Image (b). **11 Alamy Stock Photo**: Allen Creative, Steve Allen (br); Visions of America, LLC (tr). **12 Alamy Stock Photo**: State Archives of Florida / Florida Memory (b). **Bridgeman Images**: North Wind Pictures (t). **13 Alamy Stock Photo**: Granger Historical Picture Archive (c); The History Collection (t); incamerastock (bl); North Wind Picture Archives (br). **14 Alamy Stock Photo**: Lanmas (t); North Wind Picture Archives (b). **15 Alamy Stock Photo**: The Granger Collection (t); North Wind Picture Archives (b). **16 Getty Images**: MPI (t); poweroforever (b). **17 Getty Images**: Christine_Kohler (t); duncan1890 (b). **18 Alamy Stock Photo**: Imago (b). **19 Alamy Stock Photo**: Everett Collection Inc (tl). **Library of Congress, Washington, D.C.**: (tr). **20 Alamy Stock Photo**: The Color Archives (bl). **Bridgeman Images**: North Wind Pictures (tr). **21 Alamy Stock Photo**: Art Collection 3 (br); Pictorial Press Ltd (cl). **SuperStock**: Piemags / PL Photography Limited (tr). **26 Alamy Stock Photo**: Heritage Image Partnership Ltd (t); Lebrecht Music & Arts (bl). **Getty Images**: MPI (br). **27 Alamy Stock Photo**: Heritage Image Partnership Ltd (b). **Bridgeman Images**: Look and Learn (t). **28 Alamy Stock Photo**: Patrick Guenette (t). **Getty Images**: Kean Collection (bl). **29 Alamy Stock Photo**: Associated Press (cr); PSF Collection (t). **30 Alamy Stock Photo**: Colin Waters (b). **Getty Images**: KenWiedemann (t). **31 Alamy Stock Photo. 32 Alamy Stock Photo**: Associated Press (t); Chronicle (br). **Library of Congress, Washington, D.C. 33 Alamy Stock Photo**: FM Archive (br). **Courtesy of Ron Henggeler**: Artist : Tom Phillips (t). **34 Alamy Stock Photo**: North Wind Picture Archives (b); Science History Images (t). **35 Alamy Stock Photo**: Hum Images (t); M. Timothy O'Keefe (br). **Bridgeman Images**: Saint Louis Art Museum / Museum purchase (cl). **36 Alamy Stock Photo**: Anne Rippy (t). **Shutterstock.com**: JNix (b). **37 Alamy Stock Photo**: Associated Press (cl). **Getty Images**: YinYang (t). **Shutterstock.com**: eurobanks (b). **40 Alamy Stock Photo**: Granger Historical Picture Archive. **41 Alamy Stock Photo**: Djodris. **43 Alamy Stock Photo**: Xinhua. **19 Alamy Stock Photo**: North Wind Picture Archives (b).

Cover images: *Front and Back*: **Alamy Stock Photo**: M. Timothy O'Keefe c; *Front*: **Alamy Stock Photo**: Allen Creative, Steve Allen br, Universal Images Group North America LL t; **Bridgeman Images**: Look and Learn bl; **Getty Images / iStock**: Campwillowlak c; *Back*: **Alamy Stock Photo**: AAA Photostock tl; **Getty Images**: Kean Collection bl.

All the books in the DK Super History series have been reviewed by authenticity readers to ensure the represented cultures and experiences are accurate.

This book uses language as appropriate to modern contexts. Historical terms that are no longer acceptable may be present in original source materials and images. These sources are included to present authentic insights into history.